Essential Clapham

A pocket guide to the
history of Clapham – and
the best cultural and
historical sights today

Callum Moy

Essential
LONDON

First published in 2020
Essential London
13 Jessica Road
London SW18 2QL
www.essentialldn.com

British Library Cataloguing in Publication Data.
A catalogue record for this book is available from the British Library.

978 1 5272 7268 2

Typesetting in Times New Roman.
Printed in Great Britain

Mount Pond, Clapham Common

Contents

Venn Street and St Mary's Church

Introduction

Clapham is perhaps best known as the home of the 'man on the Clapham omnibus' – a term meant to represent an ordinary man, first coined in a legal case in 1903. Back then, Clapham was the archetypal commuter suburb.

In the 1960's Nairn described Clapham as having the perfect recipe for a village; consisting of shops, an open space, houses, a natural centre and even a Georgian church. Today, unlike many villages, it also has a high population of Millennials and Generation Zs - keeping the place vibrant, stylish and thriving – and arguably, no longer an 'ordinary' suburb!

Mansions at the south end of Cedars Road

Underground, Clapham Common

Historical timeline

Clapham first mentioned in the register of Chertsey Abbey

Samuel Pepys dies in Clapham

St Paul's Church opens

Manor purchased by Sir Henry Atkins

William Wilberforce moves to Clapham

| 890 | 1616 | 1703 | 1797 | 1815 |

| 1086 | 1690 | 1776 | 1805 |

First stagecoach service between Clapham and the City of London

Thomas Babington Macaulay lives, and is educated, in Clapham

Geoffrey de Mandeville becomes the first Lord of the Manor of Clapham

Holy Trinity Church opens

Roman Stone, Omnibus Theatre (from the Tower of London)

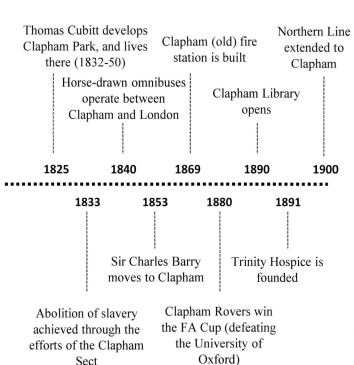

Thomas Cubitt develops Clapham Park, and lives there (1832-50)

Clapham (old) fire station is built

Northern Line extended to Clapham

Horse-drawn omnibuses operate between Clapham and London

Clapham Library opens

1825   **1840**   **1869**   **1890**   **1900**

1833   **1853**   **1880**   **1891**

Sir Charles Barry moves to Clapham

Trinity Hospice is founded

Abolition of slavery achieved through the efforts of the Clapham Sect

Clapham Rovers win the FA Cup (defeating the University of Oxford)

Holy Trinity Church (showing bomb shrapnel marks)

9

Origins and foundations

Frist mentioned in AD 880, Clapham had grown to a population of around one hundred people when it was recorded in King William's survey (for taxation) of his newly conquered lands; the Domesday Survey of 1086. The name of Clapham is thought to be derived from homestead (ham) on the hill (clop). It was popular due to its elevation overlooking the Battersea marshes and became prominent during the Roman occupation (AD43-410), being situated on the military road from London to Chichester. Known as Stane Street it ran a south west course between Clapham Common South Side and Abbeville Road.

Upon the Norman Conquest in 1066, many English landowners either fled the country or acquiesced to the transfer of their land to the Conqueror. From the outset the King owned all the land and gave large parts to his Lords, in exchange for their service. In turn, the Lord gave tenure of parcels of land to his subjects to farm, in this new French style of working, we call feudalism today. Feudal Clapham would persist until the Black Death (1346-53), when the scarcity of labour elevated the bargaining power of the working classes - and a new breed of independent yeoman farmer was born.

Holy Trinity Church, Clapham Common

After the Norman invasion, Geoffrey de Mandeville became Lord of the Manor of Clapham. The manor passed through generations of families having French heritage; the Mandevilles', Romeyns', Gowers' and Clerkes'. Bartholomew Clerke built the first Clapham Manor House in the early 1580's (remembered by the street name Turret Grove when the manor was demolished in 1840). In 1616, Henry Atkins (a physician to King James I) purchased the manor. The population of Clapham remained small (a few hundred) – many working for, and all governed by, the Lord of the Manor. From the Atkins' the manor passed to the Bowyers'. Today Lord Denham (Bertram Bowyer) is the Lord of the Manor of Clapham.

Cattle Trough, The Pavement

Mews and carriage repairs, Cedars Road

Following the Great Fire of London in 1666 (that destroyed nearly all the City's housing) Clapham was one of many villages around London to have an influx of new residents from the City. Clapham Old Town was particularly favoured, owing to its high ground and proximity to the City of London – that quickly re-started trading after the fire.

The Common was the 'waste' land belonging to the lords of the manor. In the nineteenth century, residents resisted its enclosure and in 1877 the Common was acquired by the pan-London Metropolitan Board of Works - and dedicated for use by the public.

Crescent Grove

In the eighteenth and nineteenth centuries, Clapham was ripe for the developers to move in and provide large houses suitable for merchants, politicians and professional men. The focus of the area shifted to around the Common and its spiritual nucleus; Holy Trinity Church, built in 1776.

Clapham became popular with the newly energised Evangelical Christians and was strongly associated with the slavery abolitionists, in particular, locals, William Wilberforce (Broomwood Road) and Zachary Macaulay (The Pavement).

In 1825 Thomas Cubitt developed 230 acres of Clapham Park hosting substantial mansions, of which very few survive today. The popularity of Clapham led to higher land prices, so new terraced developments replaced former mansions (e.g. Crescent Grove) alongside French (the mansions at the south of Cedars Road) and Dutch (at the southern end of The Chase) styles of architecture.

Following bomb damage, during World War II, mainly publicly-funded developments answered the call for affordable housing, but over officious schemes in the 1960's and 70's bulldozed-away much heritage, like at Clapham Park.

Abbeville Road

By 1825, stage coaches were the main method of commuting for the privileged. Ten years later, larger horse-drawn omnibuses connected Clapham and the City of London. Both modes were the preserve of the rich. Railways arrived in the 1860's, but were still costly forms of transport.

Further housing developments stimulated the need for transportation for middle-income commuters - answered by horse-drawn trams in the 1870's. And the Tube lines arrived in 1900, finally enabling lower-income workers to commute between Clapham and central London.

Today, Clapham's easy access to the West End and The City make it a very attractive (albeit pricey) residential area. It remains popular with young professionals' and older residents in a fusion of cultures and styles – quite a village!

Clapham Common

Clapham Manor Street

Essential streets

Abbeville Road, recognised as the probable route of the Roman Road from London to Chichester. Developed during the 1890s. Today, it's a popular shopping and eating-out area with a strongly local feel. The former Union of Post Office Workers is at the intersection with Crescent Lane.

Clapham Common North Side, the best preserved road around the Common with many of the original mansions and terraces still in situ; the finest examples being 29 The Elms (former home of Sir Charles Barry), 58 Bryom House (former Manor House School, c1790) and the Georgian terrace at 13-21 (original home of the African Academy, a missionary school for the sons of native African chiefs).

Clapham High Street, the original commuter thoroughfare. From 1690, it reflected progress in public transportation systems; starting with stagecoaches and much later, horse-drawn omnibuses, the railways, horse-drawn trams, the Underground and electric trams. Each stage offering more capacity and swelling the population of Clapham. It was the destination for shoppers and the grandest cinema; The Majestic - now Infernos night-club).

Abbeville Road

Clapham Common North Side

Clapham High Street

Old Town, as the name suggests, was the medieval hub of old Clapham - centered on a hill overlooking (what were the former) Battersea Marshes. It was the location of Clapham Manor House (at the intersection with Turret Grove) and, via Rectory Grove leads to the former old parish church of St Paul's. The former parish school still exists at the junction with North Street - established in 1648. The 'Queen Anne' (1702-1715) style terrace at 39-43 is one of the oldest remaining in Clapham, dating from the early 1700's. Today, Old Town is well-known for its social life, fine dining and pubs.

Elisabeth Terrace, Rectory Grove

Matrimony Place

The Pavement, the prime retail space of the 1800's, connecting the transport terminuses in Old Town and Clapham Common Underground stations. Fine original shopfronts attest to the days of high-end shopping and personal service (Common, at 16 The Pavement, retains the original counters and cases from Henry Deane's 1837 Chemist shop)

Venn Street, home to Clapham's earliest cinema (the Electric Palace, 1910) and its current cinema (Clapham Picturehouse) is also popular for its Saturday market and evening party atmosphere. Named after the Rector of Clapham (from 1792) – and whose grandson created the Venn diagram.

The Pavement

Venn Street

Three famous residents

There have been many notable residents of Clapham. But here is a top three that have spent more extensive time in Clapham.

Samuel Pepys, moved to a house on Clapham Common North Side in 1700 and died there three years later. He is best remembered for his voluminous, revealing coded-diaries (covering the period 1600 to 1669) that described the affairs of the day, his own frank opinions of others and his sexual infidelities – that would get you locked up today! What is often forgotten is that after The Restoration of the Monarchy in 1660, he reached the highest levels of government administration at the Navy Board, a fact making the diaries all that more insightful and remarkable. The house in Clapham belonged to his former clerk and assistant William Hewer, with whom Pepys lived for his last three years.

Clapham Common North Side

Cock Pond, Clapham Common

William Wilberforce was the driving force of the Clapham Sect, a group of evangelical Christians that successfully campaigned to drive parliament into passing a bill abolishing the slave trade (in 1807) and slavery altogether in British Dominions (in 1833). Born in Hull, the son of a wealthy merchant (and grandson of the mayor) he became an independent MP - but it was his conversion to an evangelical Christian that resulted in lifelong changes. Sadly, Wilberforce died only three days before the 1833 bill was passed. He lived Broomwood Road at the intersection with Wroughton Road, where a plaque bears evidence.

Sir Charles Barry shot to acclaim after winning the competition to rebuild the Houses of Parliament with a gothic design, favoured by the panel as proper English (as distinct from classical) architecture, befitting our heritage. Barry moved to The Elms at 29 Clapham Common North Side. The building stands today.

On the site behind this
house stood until 1904
Broomwood House (for-
merly Broomfield) where
WILLIAM WILBERFORCE
resided during the
CAMPAIGN against
SLAVERY which he
successfully conducted
in Parliament

Broomwood Road

The Elms, Clapham Common North Side

Other remarkable citizens

Thomas Babington Macaulay, a child prodigy schooled in Clapham, Whig statesman and eminent historian. Macaulay Road is named after him. He lived at 5 The Pavement.

Henry Cavendish, wealthy reclusive scientist (and nephew of the 3rd Duke of Devonshire), he proved that water was a compound. The Cavendish Laboratory in Cambridge is named after him. Lived at Cavendish House (now gone), situated on the south side of Cavendish Road.

John Frances Bentley, designed the Roman Catholic Westminster Cathedral in Victoria Street, London. Lived at 43 Old Town in a fine Queen Anne style House, dating from the early 1700's.

The Pavement

39-43 Old Town

The Clapham Sect, a group of rich, male Christian evangelists who campaigned remarkably to reform social and moral standards and to abolish slavery in British Dominions (achieved in 1833). Led by William Wilberforce and Zachary Macaulay and included Henry Venn, John Thornton, Granville Sharp and others. Meetings centered on Holy Trinity Church, Clapham

Benjamin Franklin, a frequent visitor to Clapham (whilst the colonial agent for the Pennsylvania Assembly) in order to experiment with surface chemistry on the ponds of Clapham Common. One of the five who signed the Declaration of Independence of the United States. Lived in Craven Street, Westminster

Entrance gates to Holy Trinity Church

Mount Pond, Clapham Common

Thomas Cubitt, speculative developer and master builder, best known for his Belgravia development for the Duke of Westminster (the Grosvenor family). Responsible for the (largely gone) mansions of the Clapham Park estate. Built many of the houses in Clapham Manor Street, including The Bread and Roses pub. Lived in a self-built mansion (now gone) on Clarence Avenue.

John Doulton, founder of a ceramics business that grew (with his son) into Royal Doulton. Lived at 81 Clapham Common North Side.

William Edgar, department store magnate in partnership with George Swan. Lived at Eagle House, where you can see a part of the remaining south wing at the top of Narbonne Road.

Stanley Gibbons, world-renowned philatelist who employed a small staff at, and issued a catalogue of stamps for sale from, 45 (formerly 25) The Chase, where he lived briefly

Edvard Greig, leading Norwegian romantic composer and conductor, who preferred to stay in Clapham when performing in London. Stayed at 47 Clapham Common North Side

Cubitt Terrace

Doulton House, Clapham Common North Side

Graham Greene, a leading English novelist of the twentieth century. Wrote the 'End of the Affair', set in Clapham, whilst living at 14 Clapham Common North Side.

Marie Kendall, music hall star who spent nearly six decades touring the music halls of Britain, France and America - and topping the bill at the 1932 Royal Variety Performance. Retired to Clapham Common North Side for twenty-five years before her death at the age of 91 years old

John Newton Mappin, founder of Mappin & Webb, the stylish West End department store. Lived in Clapham Park.

Natsume Soseki, considered one of the greatest writers in Japanese history. Characteristically, all his works were sombre works and his last novel, Grass on the Wayside written in 1915, was autobiographical. Lived at 61 The Chase.

Vivienne Westwood, the iconoclastic genius of fashion has lived in Clapham for much of her life and is active on local matters. Created DBE in 2006. Lives on Clapham Common North Side.

Former home of Graham Greene, Clapham Common North Side

Clapham Common

The beating heart and rich green lung of Clapham – its 220 acres provide rest, recreation and an open-air concert venue for the people of Clapham and south London. Thackeray eulogized 'of all the pretty suburbs that still adorn our Metropolis there are few that exceed in charm Clapham Common'. And like many of London's green spaces, it has served multiple purposes that are lost on us today - home to army training, allotments, American Indian 'medicine shows', pre-fab post-war housing - and anti-aircraft guns.

In feudal times, the workers of the manor had rights to graze animals and collect fruit and wood. Drained and laid-out in 1722, its raucous annual fair was banned in 1781. Bare-knuckle fighting, hopping matches and general (alcohol induced) excesses were not to the liking of residents around the common. Today, annual fairs are limited to three per year!

Clapham Common with the mansions at south end of Cedars Road

Long Pond, Clapham Common and the spire of St Mary's Church

The Duke of Cumberland's army camped here in 1745, the year of the Jacobite Rebellion, to return later that year with convicted Jacobites, eight of whom met a nasty fate at the gallows in nearby Kennington.

The remaining four ponds on the common were purpose built (in the eighteenth century), not for their aesthetic beauty but to get at the underlying gravel for road building. Never the less, they have a special place in scientific history, being used by Benjamin Franklin for his experiments in surface chemistry.

In 1871, when the common was under threat of enclosure (for private use of, and development by, the Lord of the Manor), it was acquired by the London Metropolitan Board of Works and dedicated for use by the public, evermore.

In 1809 the famous bandstand was erected. Refurbished in 2006 it is still London's largest, hosting summer concerts, parents, buggies and toddlers.

Bandstand, Clapham Common

Grand designs

Crescent Grove. Clapham Common South Side once hosted a series of grand mansions facing the common, but it has suffered under the knife of post-war development more than North Side. One startling exception is the hidden beauty of Crescent Grove, described by Pevsner as a 'handsome crescent'. It is late Georgian, designed by Francis Child as a family investment and built in 1824. It requires little imagination to see the Hansom cabs (cab from cabriolet) plying in and out of the grove. The central gardens were once enclosed with railings, but are now watched over by its proud and protective residents, who are responsible for its upkeep. Child kept most of the grove to members of his family, but he must have liked his crackers; number 26 was leased to the industrialist John Carr - founder of the water biscuit and Peak Frean & Co.

South Buildings, Clapham Common South Side

Crescent Grove

Grafton Square, nearer to Old Town is an early Victorian town square, quite unique in south London - being more familiar in fashionable Kensington at the time. This large garden square was completed in 1851, with central communal gardens for residents to perambulate. (Within twenty years, the green-finger bug had taken grip of the country and house purchasers would demand private gardens in the future).

In 1927 the gardens became a private tennis club, before being purchased by the local authority in 1953. Today, Lambeth Parks ensures the square, and its recreational facilities, are free for all to use.

Grafton Square

Grafton Square

The Orangery, an astonishing find in Clapham is this orangery (so called for its use as a winter store for valued plants and flowers) located, rather incongruously, in the heart of the 1950's Notre Dame Estate. If any proof was needed of the original grandeur of the mansions of Clapham, here it is. The original house, built in 1740 by Robert Thornton, a wealthy merchant from Yorkshire, has gone - demolished in 1945. But the Orangery (dating 1793) survives. Along with its gardens and lake it was a favourite with Queen Charlotte (wife of King George III). In 1800, the Orangery was decked out to host Prime Minister William Pitt (the Younger) and his cabinet.

The Orangery, Worsopp Drive

The Underground, Clapham is unique on the Underground network in having three stations to its name on the Northern Line - London's first all-electric tube line. The line was extended to Clapham North and Clapham Common in 1900 and Clapham South was opened in 1926. Four men that contributed, more than most, to the success of the 'Tube' were Frank Pick (MD in the 1920's and admired for his influence on design and operations), Charles Holden (who designed many of the stations in the 1920's – including Clapham South), Harry Beck (who designed the present London Underground Tube map in 1931 – by applying the principles of wiring diagrams). And not forgetting, Sir Marc Brunel who in 1843 constructed the world's first rail tunnel under a river; beneath the River Thames between Rotherhithe and Wapping (still in use today).

Underground, Clapham Common Station

Underground, Clapham Common Station

Historical buildings

Deane & Co, established on The Pavement in 1837, the year Queen Victoria's accession, it was one London's oldest pharmacies until it ceased trading in 1986.   Today, it is Common, a café. It retains the original furnishings, cabinets and drawers, which along with the Georgian building, are all Grade II listed.

Eagle House, Clapham's largest mansion and grounds (according to the 1870 OS map of Clapham) it is all but gone, bar the perfectly visible south wing at the top of Narbonne Avenue. It was home to William Edgar (of the west-end department store Swan and Edgar).

Clapham Library, with money flooding-in to government coffers from international trade, abundant libraries sprung-up across London in the late nineteenth century. Clapham's opened, at the intersection of Old Town and Orlando Road, in 1889 sporting Flemish Renaissance decoration. In 2012, a lively campaign was mobilised by locals, successfully preventing its demolition. Sitting opposite Clapham's main bus terminus – it's now the appropriately named, Omnibus Theatre.

Deane's Chemist, The Pavement

Eagle House (south wing), Narbonne Road

Majestic Cinema, opening in the High Street in 1914 it was Clapham's grandest cinema, seating 3000 people and home to a resident symphony orchestra. Later in its life, it doubled up as a bingo-hall before closing in 1960 due to falling audiences. Today it's Infernos.

The Old Court House, at 43 Netherford Road functioned both as a court house and a standards and testing office for Clapham from 1901. It resulted from the creation of the London County Council (the elected body responsible for running much of London's public services from 1889). It's now a Grade II listed private residence.

Majestic Cinema, Clapham High Street

Old Court House, Netherford Road

The Old Fire Station, is the building with two doorways opposite the Old Town pub. Since 1707, every parish was legally required to operate a fire station, to provide a service to houses without fire insurance. The standards varied, but at least the days of 'no fire insurance plaque, no service' had gone. By 1866, the Metropolitan Fire Brigade (MFB) was formed (by amalgamating the brigades operated by private insurance companies). This building was purpose-built for the MFB in 1869 and is a private residence today.

Clapham Parochial School, the building at the apex of North Street and Rectory Grove was the parish school, established in 1812. It had one large room. The school practised the Monitorial System (adopting the motto 'he who teaches, learns'), whereby older pupils tutored younger pupils. 'Excessive prize giving' was used to both control and reward pupils - the system fell out of favour when it was realised that trained teachers were probably better!. At the top of Macaulay Road still stands the annex to the original school in Old Town – now a private residence.

Old Fire Station, The Pavement

Clapham Parochial School, Old Town

Clapham Parochial School (annex), Macaulay Road

Royal Trinity Hospice, walking the sweep of buildings starting with Trinity Hospice at 30 Clapham Common North Side, along Church Terrace and running down to the library at Orlando Road, is one of Clapham's most attractive and historic perambulations. The mansion was purchased by the Hoare banking family and, with donations following an appeal in The Times newspaper, opened in 1891 as a home for the terminally ill. It is the UK's oldest hospice.

Temperance Billiard Hall, at 47 Clapham High Street is a reminder of the influence of the temperance movement at the turn of the century. An enterprising Lancashire company (The Temperance Billiard Hall Company) built numerous halls across London. Now an architectural practice, at least no alcohol is being sold on the premises, unlike its cousins in Clapham Junction and Fulham – the latter ironically named The Temperance.

Royal Trinity Hospice, Clapham Common North Side

Temperance Billiard Hall, Clapham High Street

Monuments, statues and markers

Boundary markers, dotted throughout Clapham are parish boundary markers, delineating Clapham from Wandsworth and Battersea. The history of Clapham's local government is beyond the scope of this short book, but here are the basics from the first mention of Clapham in AD 800. At that time, Clapham belonged to Surrey and was believed to be governed by Aelfrid - appointed by the king (of either the Sussex or Kent Saxons). During the Viking invasions, governance in the south, flip-flopped between the Vikings and Saxons between 1013 and 1042. Upon the Norman Conquest in 1066, the Conqueror installed his own man (Geoffrey de Mandeville) – and so began 500 years of medieval feudalism in Clapham - headed by the hereditary Lord of the Manor of Clapham.

Boundary markers for the parishes of Battersea and Clapham (Wix's Lane)

The Tudors created comprehensive and formal Church of England parishes - led by vestries, a system of early local government. The 'local' Surrey parishes were Battersea, Clapham, Putney, Tooting, Streatham and Wandsworth. Vestry-led government continued through to the mid-nineteenth century when the need for standardisation and efficiency led to the creation of The Metropolitan Board of Works (MBW) in 1855, then the London County Council in 1889 and the GLC in 1965. In 1986, autonomy was handed to the boroughs, supported (from 2000) on London-wide strategic matters by the Greater London Authority, led by The Mayor of London.

The Victorian, iron post, boundary markers still fulfil a purpose today - Clapham straddles the London Boroughs of Lambeth and Wandsworth

Day-light robbery, so went the saying at the governments tax on windows in the eighteenth and nineteenth centuries. So new homes were built with many windows bricked-up, should the tax ever be repealed - which it was in 1851. There are some fine examples in Clapham!

Elms Road, Clapham Common South Side

Temperance Statue, the drinking fountain near The Pavement was originally erected in 1884 by the Temperance Society, located in offices near London Bridge. It had to be removed fifteen years later when its weight threatened the structural integrity of the bridge. It shows a woman offering water to a man – a sentiment no doubt lost on the evening revellers in any of the pubs along the Pavement and Old Town!

Clock Tower, was unveiled with great civic pride at the top of the High Street in 1906. It is made from materials that last, Portland Stone and Aberdeen granite. Sadly, the mechanism itself has not proved as long lasting, having given up the ghost in 1964. Thickening of the walls left no room to get at the mechanism. So there is stands, in a prominent position outside Clapham Common tube station, reading the correct time twice a day!

Temperance Statue, Clapham Common

Clock Tower, Clapham High Street

Four places of worship

Holy Trinity, on the north east of the common is a church renowned throughout the world as the nucleus for the debates and sermons (led by its evangelical rector, John Venn) which were the impetus for the abolition of slavery in British Dominions in 1833. It was an initiative of local evangelical Christians led by: William Wilberforce (Broomwood Road), Granville Sharp (Clapham Common North Side), Zachary Macaulay (The Pavement), John Thornton (Clapham Common South Side) and others recorded on a plaque on the south exterior wall. The church opened in June 1776 – one month before the United States Declaration of Independence. Built on land donated by the last member of the Atkins family to be the Lord of the Manor of Clapham, it is designed in the classical style; popular before Gothic Revival became the standard church-building template from 1850 – and to differentiate Britain from the US Federal style of classical architecture!

Holy Trinity Church, Clapham Common

St Paul's Church, situated at the end of Rectory Grove, opened for worship in September 1815 - being only three months after the Battle of Waterloo, this victory would surely have featured in the opening sermon.   Such was the popularity of church-going, the church was built to provide overflow capacity for Holy Trinity, built forty years earlier . Inside, the most important monument is that to Sir Richard Atkins, Lord of the Manor, and his family dating from 1689. The site of St Paul's is that of the original old Clapham parish church. Old St Paul's was demolished in around 1776, mainly due to its small size and condition – but its remote location from the faithful around the Common would have contributed to its demise.

St Paul's Church, Rectory Grove

Allotments, Rectory Grove

St Mary's Church, completed in 1851, Clapham's Our Lady of Victories church on Clapham Park Road is one of the best Victorian churches in south London (according to Pevsner). It was designed by William Wardell, pupil to Augustus Pugin - gifted assistant to Charles Barry's designs for the new Houses of Parliament, that opened in 1852.

Oddfellows Hall, was opened in Belmont Close for the Ebenezer Strict Baptists in 1852, it moved around the corner within a few years, to a new chapel; the Ebenezer Strict Baptist Chapel (still serving the community). Oddfellows was a 'friendly society' – an association of like minds that provided financial or social services in the days before the NHS and modern insurance.

St Mary's Church, Clapham Park Road

Oddfellows Hall, Belmont Road

Clapham at war

Anti-aircraft battery, the two areas of tarmacked-over ground on the north-west side of the common are the raised surrounds for the World War II 3.7in gun batteries, that searched the skies for enemy bombers. Above the batteries, silver barrage balloons prevented enemy fighters from getting too close.   Bombing intensified after the Battle of Britain (July – Oct 1940), Hitler having given up the prospect of a land invasion – and continued to May 1941 in an attempt to break the morale of the British. There was a lull in bombing until 1944, when the V1 (Luftwaffe) 'doodlebug' and V2 (German army) rocket terrified the population – the former, noisy upon approach and frightening once their engine cut-out, the latter deadly silent up to the last second.   According to www.bombsight.org, 53 High Explosive Bombs were dropped on Clapham – targeted on the most populated areas.

Concrete base of former AA battery, Clapham Common (north west)

Deep level air-raid shelters, Clapham is home to three sites (of five across south London) owing to the course of the Northern Line and its three stations – all entrances are visible by their concrete circular ventilation shafts opposite the stations. At first, the tube lines themselves were used for shelter, but by Oct 1940 construction was underway at three sites; Clapham North, Clapham Common and Clapham South and completed by Sep 1942. Each shelter was around 400 metres in length and could accommodate 6,000 people in bunks. However, in effect, the shelters arrived too late, since enemy bombing had ceased by May 1941 – so the shelters were re-purposed as troop 'hotels' until the start the V1/V2 campaigns in 1944. In 1948, Clapham South shelter provided the first accommodation for around 240 immigrants arriving from Jamaica on the Empire Windrush – and later as overflow accommodation for various occasions, including the Festival of Britain in 1951. Today, you can visit the Clapham South shelter, visit www.ltmuseum.co.uk.

Deep level shelter, Clapham High Street

Deep level shelter, Clapham South

Living like a local

Omnibus Theatre, 1 Clapham Common North Side, London SW4 0QW. Tel: 020 7498 4699 / www.omnibus-clapham.org
Occupying the old library in Old Town, the Omnibus has rapidly become an institution in the short time since opening in 2013. Its affordable programme of re-imagined classics, contemporary storytelling, new writing and interdisciplinary work has led to multiple awards. Its café is airy, well provisioned and a unique alternative to the chains.

London Russian Ballet School, 42 Clapham Manor St, Clapham, London SW4 6DZ. Tel: 020 7498 0498 / www.classicalballet.org
The ballet school is based in another of Thomas Cubitt's Clapham designs - this one completed in 1854.   For talented and aspiring pupils, it offers vocational (age 14-19) and pre-vocational (age 9-15) training in the Russian Classical Ballet syllabus.

Omnibus Theatre (former Clapham Library), Old Town

Russian Ballet School, Clapham Manor Street

Clapham Picture House, 76 Venn St, Clapham Town, London SW4 0AT. Tel: 0871 902 5747 / www.picturehouses.com/cinema/clapham-picturehouse

Clapham's newest picture house rubs shoulders with the building that housed one of Clapham's first cinemas; the Electric Palace Cinema, that opened in 1910 on the corner of the High Street and Venn Street. The Clapham Picture House is an independent arthouse cinema with a café, bar and restaurant – serving up salads, burgers and classic pies. The cinema shows mainstream, classic and cult films – as well as independents, documentaries and foreign language releases.

Italia Conti, 72 Landor Rd, Larkhall, London SW9 9PH. Tel: 020 7733 3210 / www.italiaconti.com

With alumina ranging from Sir Noel Coward to Russell Brand, Italia Conti is the world's oldest theatre arts training school, founded in 1911. Today, it is the leading Performing Arts institution in the country, specialising in musical theatre, acting and dance.

Clapham Picture House, Venn Street

Clapham Leisure Centre, 141 Clapham Manor Street, Clapham, Lambeth. London SW4 6DB. Tel: 020 7627 7900 / www.better.org.uk/leisure-centre/london/lambeth/claphamleisurecentre
A jewel in Clapham's crown is the modern leisure centre opened in 2012; comprising two pools, a fitness centre, sports hall and badminton courts – with a variety of fitness classes and courses.

Clapham Library, Mary Seacole Centre, 91 Clapham High Street, London SW4 7DB. Tel: 020 7926 0717 /
www.lambeth.gov.uk/places/clapham-library
Remembering the brave service of the Jamaican-born, mixed race nurse who cared for the sick and wounded soldiers of the Crimean War, (but whose service was overlooked by the War Office at the time) the library, in the centre bearing her name, opened in 2012. It was Lambeth's first self-service library and offers the usual services plus access to computers, free Wi-Fi and a stunning performance space for hire.

Studio Voltaire, 1A Nelsons Row, Clapham Town, London SW4 7JR. Tel; 020 7622 1294 /
www.studiovoltaire.org
Studio Voltaire is a non-profit gallery and artist studios based in Clapham, South London. The organisation focuses on contemporary arts, staging a celebrated public programme of exhibitions, performances, and live events.

Clapham Leisure Centre, Clapham Manor Street

Essential pubs and cafes

The Alexandra, 14 Clapham Common South Side, Clapham Common, London SW4 7AA. Tel: 020 7627 5102 / www.alexandraclapham.com
The Alexandra Hotel, with its famous first-floor restaurant, was built in 1866. It was a vast hotel that originally included the buildings that flank it on either side. Today, it's original Victorian wrap-round bar and features make it a popular night out, particularly good for fans of sport.

The Bread and Roses, 68 Clapham Manor St, Clapham Town, London SW4 6DZ. Tel: 020 7498 1779 / www.breadandrosespub.com
Designed and built by Thomas Cubitt, it is the only building in the street of his own design.   Originally named The Bowyer Arms, after the Lord of the Manor, it was renamed The Bread & Roses in remembrance of the women textile workers who campaigned for better conditions in Massachusetts, USA in 1912 – they carried banners calling for 'bread and roses'. It's a large airy pub, with a platform to host the regular shows and performances. Photographs of pop stars, concert venues and political memorabilia adorn the walls – giving it the feel of a student bar. It's an award-winning free-house, which prides itself as a pub with a social consciousness.

The Alexandra, Clapham Common South Side

Bread and Roses, Clapham Manor Street

The Bobbin, 1-3 Lillieshall Rd, Clapham Town, London SW4 0LN / Tel: 020 7738 8953 / www.thebobbinclapham.com
Situated in a terrace of early nineteenth century houses, The Bobbin is, arguably, one of the best neighbourhood pub's in Clapham. It offers a modern Italian-influenced menu and has a tranquil beer garden.

The Clapham North, 409 Clapham Rd, Larkhall, London SW9 9BT.   Tel: 020 7274 2472 / www.theclaphamnorth.co.uk
A contemporary feel inside a late Georgian building with exposed brickwork, booth seating and an outside area. Serving fine food, making a speciality of brunch at the weekend. There is a very popular quiz on Sunday nights.

The Clapham Tap, 128 Clapham Manor St, Clapham Town, London SW4 6ED.   Tel: 020 7498 9633 / www.the-clapham-tap.business.site
A snug pre-1830's building, offering a wide range of hand-pumped beers, having a fine, long, garden hosting table-tennis and Boules.

The Bobbin, Lillieshall Road

The Clapham North, Clapham Road

The Clapham Tap, Clapham Manor Street

Common, 17 The Pavement, Clapham Town, London SW4 0HY.   www.wearecommon.co.uk
Occupying the Grade II listed building of the former, long-established, Chemist Henry Deane, the original cabinets and boxes ensure it retains the feel of a Victorian chemists. A gift shop and bulk pantry staples fill out one side of this trendy café serving coffee and light bites.

The Falcon, 33 Bedford Rd, Larkhall, London SW4 7SQ.   Tel: 020 7274 2428 / www.thefalconclapham.co.uk
The Falcon's quirky charm, located next to Clapham North tube station, is the setting for a memorable drinking and dining experience with a welcoming atmosphere.

Landor Pub and Theatre, 70 Landor Rd, Larkhall, London SW9 9PH.   Tel: 020 7737 3419 / www.thelandorpub.com
A haven for locals, the Landor has a laid back and welcoming atmosphere. The historic Landor Pub and Theatre is at the forefront of fringe productions – hosting events like the Edinburgh warm-up comedy festival.

Common, The Pavement

No. 32 The Old Town, 32 The Pavement, Clapham Town, London SW4 0JE.   Tel: 020 3535 0910 / www.no32theoldtown.co.uk
With a prime location and balcony overlooking the Common, No. 32 The Old Town is a lively hang-out for Clapham fashionistas, with cool DJ soundtracks on Friday and Saturday evenings. Particularly popular for long weekend lunches.

O'Neill's Clapham, 196 Clapham High St, Clapham Town, London SW4 7UD.   Tel: 020 7498 4931 / www.oneills.co.uk/national-search/london/clapham
Originally The Plough Inn, it is one of Clapham's oldest pubs having been an eighteenth century coaching inn. The mock Tudor front was added in 1930. Today, its Irish theme ensures you'll enjoy the craic, live music, sport or a cosy meal.

Prince of Wales, 38 Old Town, Clapham Town, London SW4 0LB.   Tel: 020 7622 4964 / www.powsw4.com
An ever-popular quirky Old Town pub, serving local workers, commuters and local residents since opening in 1884. The ceiling shows off an eclectic display of object d'art, nautical themed collectables and curios that make fascinating talking points. Since 1979, all under the stewardship of Clapham's longest serving landlord.

No. 32 Old Town, The Pavement

O'Neills, Clapham High Street

The Railway, 18 Clapham High St, Clapham Town, London SW4 7UR.   Tel: Phone: 020 7622 4077 / www. therailwayclapham.co.uk
Pubs were initially built on corner-plots as accommodation for the builders – and then terraces were built in each direction from the corner. The Railway is a good example of this Victorian building technique. Known for vintage character, individuality, an off-beat edge and its convenient location opposite Clapham High Street Overground and Clapham North stations. The large dining room on the first floor is pure Victoriana.

The Rectory, 87 Rectory Grove, Clapham Town, London SW4 0DR.   Tel: 020 7622 4019 / www.therectoryclapham.co.uk
Another of Clapham's oldest pubs, tucked away in the heart of the Old Town. It's airy and cavernous interior makes it a pleasure to watch rugby and sports on the big screen. The pub has a reputation for the tastiest freshly prepared food and entertainment – welcoming the entire family and dogs.

The Stonhouse, 165 Stonhouse St, Clapham Town, London SW4 6BJ.   Tel: 020 7819 9312 / www.thestonhouse.co.uk
Off the beaten track, away from the bustle of Clapham High Street the light ambience of The Stonhouse makes an outstanding setting for its wide-range of cask ales and superb wines alongside a modern European brasserie style menu – with vegan and vegetarian dishes that could convince the staunchest of carnivores.

The Railway, Clapham High Street

The Sun, 47 Old Town, Clapham Town, London SW4 0JL.   Tel: 020 7622 4980 / www.thesunclapham.co.uk

The Sun has occupied this site since the early nineteenth century, this pub was re-built in 1880. The pub closely avoided destruction by Second World War bombing that fated the adjacent church. Today, the Sun offers a stylish drinking and dining experience with fine food, an explorative drinks menu and an authentic, homely atmosphere. Its first-floor dining room is a well-preserved Victorian example – so unique to Britain.

The Windmill, Windmill Dr, Clapham Common, London SW4 9DE.   Tel: 020 8673 4578 / www.windmillclapham.co.uk

Another of Clapham's oldest pubs, formerly the site of a windmill and then a coaching inn with extensive horse stabling. There was a pond close-by, which was filled in during the late nineteenth century to make way for the residences adjacent to the pub today. The Windmill is a quintessentially British pub, serving traditional pub classics and vegan dishes. Its proximity to the tube stations makes its boutique country-style hotel rooms very popular.

The Windmill, Clapham Common South Side

The Sun, Old Town

Credits, references and further reading

Bailey, K. *Old Ordnance Survey Maps, Clapham Common, 1870, Sheet 115* (Consett: Alan Godfrey Maps)

Bailey, K. *Old Ordnance Survey Maps, Battersea and Clapham, 1870, Sheet 101* (Consett: Alan Godfrey Maps)

Clegg, G. (1998) *Clapham past* (London: Historical Publications)

Glinert, E. (2012) *The London compendium* (London: Penguin, first pub.2003)

Green, M. (2008) *Historic Clapham* (Stroud: History Press)

Nairn, I. (2014) *Nairn's London* (London: Penguin, first pub. 1966)

Pevsner, N. and Cherry, B. (2002), *The Buildings of England, London 2: South* (London: Yale UP)

Weinreb, B. Hibbert, C et al (2008) *The London Encyclopaedia* (London: Macmillan)

Wilson, A (ed.) (2000) *The buildings of Clapham* (London: The Clapham Society)

Wilson, A. and Fry, C. (2015) *Clapham through time* (Stroud: Amberley)

www.claphamsociety.com - community, conservation and historical society

www.thisisclapham.co.uk - business and community association

Prince of Wales, Old Town

St Clair, The Pavement (Cevicheria & Wine Bar)

Holy Trinity Church

Trinity, The Polygon (Michelin Star Restaurant)

The Falcon, Bedford Road

The Rectory, Rectory Grove

Clapham Books, The Pavement

M. Moen & Sons, The Pavement

Advertisement, Lambourn Road

Café, Clapham Common

Skateboard park, Clapham Common

Former Electric Palace Cinema, Clapham High Street

Minnow, The Pavement (restaurant)